THE Great YORKSHIRE JOKE BOOK

VOL. 1

Written and compiled by
Adrian Braddy

Over 230 hilarious jokes, puns and tall tales

Dalesman

Published in Great Britain in 2018 by Dalesman
an imprint of
Country Publications Ltd
The Gatehouse, Skipton Castle, Skipton BD23 1AL
www.dalesman.co.uk
© Adrian Braddy 2018
Additional material © copyright holders as stated 2018
ISBN: 978-1-85568-372-3

Printed in China for Latitude Press Ltd.

Introduction

To the outsider, Yorkshire folk may seem dour and not easily moved, but hiding beneath that shield of Tyke steel lies a keen sense of humour.

Yorkshire wit is often joyously self-deprecating. We delight in poking fun at our supposed characteristics – stinginess, love of drink, superiority, etc.

We also love nothing more than to gently rib our near neighbours – particularly those on the wrong side of the Pennines.

And, of course, the Yorkshire humour can be pretty blunt. Banter between friends and colleagues is almost a regional sport.

In this collection of Yorkshire gags, puns and tall stories, you'll find all areas of Tyke humour are covered. There are one or two old classics, and some gags you'll have never heard before. Hopefully most of them will make you laugh, or at least raise a groan.

And if they don't, there's always Volume Two!

Adrian Braddy

North Yorkshire Police revealed details of genuine calls made to the non-emergency 101 number. In one instance, a resident from an unidentified North Yorkshire village rang to report a suspicious Tesco delivery van. When the operator asked what was suspicious about the van, the caller replied, "people in this village don't shop at Tesco".

Teacher to pupil at Swaledale primary school: "I asked you to draw a sheep eating grass while I was out of the room, but you've only drawn a sheep." Pupil: "Aye, Miss, but tha were out of t' classroom so long, t' sheep et all t' grass."

At an auction in Leeds, a wealthy American visitor announced he had lost his wallet containing £10,000 and would give a reward of £100 to the person who found it. From the back of the hall a broad Yorkshire voice shouted, "And Ah'll give thee £150!"

"As a child growing up in a grey-skied Yorkshire village, I would occasionally happen upon a Bollywood movie on the television. After a few minutes watching a bunch of sari-clad dancers cavorting on a Swiss mountain to tuneless music, I would switch over to some proper drama about housing estates and single mothers."

Simon Beaufoy

Did you hear about the dalesman who was so tight he wouldn't buy his wife a pearl necklace for their anniversary? He got her a length of baler twine and told her to start a collection.

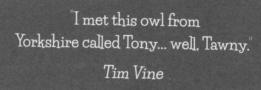

"I met this owl from Yorkshire called Tony... well, Tawny."

Tim Vine

Wrigley's has a brand new website where you can purchase all of its products. It's called ebuygum.com.

"Me an' t' missus often laugh about 'ow competitive we are... but I laugh more."

Jim had become a bit hard of hearing but he didn't want to pay for a hearing aid. So he bought a piece of flex, put one end in his top pocket and the other end in his ear. It didn't help his hearing but people spoke to him more loudly.

Did you hear about the dalesman who was so tight he used to give his children £1 each instead of an evening meal? He charged them £2 for breakfast.

It is a week before Christmas and two young brothers from Leeds are spending the night at their grandparents' house in Bedale. At 7.30pm, their grandma announces, "Time for bed, you two. Pop upstairs and say your prayers, then I'll come up and tuck you in."

As the pair kneel down beside their beds, the younger of the brothers begins praying at the top of his voice, "Dear Lord, please ask Father Christmas to bring me a mountain bike".

"Why are you shouting so loud?" the older brother hisses, nudging him. "God isn't deaf." "I know," comes the reply, "but Grandma is!"

Sign at a Yorkshire golf course: "Members will refrain from picking up lost balls until they have stopped rolling."

A Dales farmer is in Northallerton to buy his wife a Valentine's gift. Having selected a long flannel nightie with a nice floral pattern, the farmer heads for the checkout. In front of him in the queue is a young man also shopping for his other half. He is purchasing a delicate, hardly-there lacy black negligée. The farmer seemingly can't take his eyes off this flimsy nightgown, staring at it until he comes to be served. When it's his turn, the farmer steps forward and asks the shop assistant, "'As tha got owt in black flannel?"

"Ah'm strugglin' ter lose weight... Ah've got fillings in mi teeth and t' fridge magnets keep pullin' mi into t' kitchen."

Shortly after the remains of Richard III were found in a Leicester car park, archaeologists collected the bones together and drove them away in a battered old van. As the van left the car park, a voice was heard to cry, "A hearse, a hearse. My kingdom for a hearse!"

Alf swallowed all the tiles from his Scrabble set after a game with his wife turned nasty. Doctors at the local hospital said the problem would eventually work itself out, but not in so many words.

tyke top 20

Yorkshire has spawned many great songs – *On Ilkla Moor Baht 'at*, *Scarboro' Fair*, *Agadoo* – but do you ever find yourself listening to the radio and musing "It's just not Yorkshire enough"? To make amends, we've compiled the Tyke Top 20.

1 **ALL THE DINGLE LADIES** – Beyoncé

2 **LEYBURN BABY BURN** – Ash

3 **MYSTERIOUS GOOLE** – Peter Andre

4 **BITTER T' DEVIL THA KNOWS** – Kylie Minogue

5 **ROLL WHIPPET** – Oasis

6 **CAN'T LET YOU TEES ME** – Commodores

7 **WALKING IN THE AIRE** – Aled Jones

\\

Sign spotted in a Leeds baker's window: "Cakes like your mother used to make, £2.50. Cakes like she thought she used to make, £5."

On a bitterly cold February morning, a man is fishing at a partly frozen beck in Upper Wharfedale, with no success. After a while, a boy arrives and starts fishing himself, a little further upstream. Within minutes he catches a huge brown trout. To the man's astonishment, just five minutes later, he lands another. This continues apace, with fish after fish being pulled from the stream, and after a while the man can contain his curiosity no longer. He walks up the beck and asks the boy what his secret is. "Yu hf tu kp yr wms wm," the youngster replies. "Sorry? I didn't catch that," says the man, at which point the boy turns and spits something into a bucket. "I said, 'yer have ter keep yer worms warm'."

"Founded on textiles, until 1969 Leeds had the world's largest surviving woollen mill. Then someone pulled a loose thread and the whole building unravelled." – *Humphrey Lyttelton*, I'm Sorry I Haven't A Clue

"Ower mam has a new toaster," a small boy tells his friend. "It's reet clever. When t' toast is done, a bell rings." "Ower ma's toaster's better," says his friend. "When t' toast's ready, it sends out smoke signals."

A rambler is walking in a northern dale one sunny morning when he comes upon a wizened old chap, who appears to the walker as much a part of the countryside as the drystone wall he is leaning against. "Nah then," the man mumbles by way of a greeting. "Oh, good afternoon," exclaims the earnest walker, catching his breath. After a long pause, the elderly sage grabs a few strands of grass in his fist and stares at them intently, before letting them blow away in the wind. A few more awkward moments of silence later, he declares, "Happen it'll be teemin' dahn later." "Oh really, it's going to rain?" the walker asks. "And you can tell that just by looking at a blade of grass?" he adds, visibly impressed. "Nay lad," the man replies. "Ah heard it on t' wireless."

Eric was very excited that he had finished his jigsaw in only six months, because on the box it said, "From two to four years".

Screen Break

The flowers of Yorkshire are like the women of Yorkshire. Every stage of their growth has its own beauty, but the last phase is always the most glorious. Then very quickly they all go to seed.

Quote from the 2003 film
Calendar Girls

BAINBRIDGE ENGLISH
DICTIONARY

You know those words that simply don't sound like what they ought to mean? For decades, the team behind BBC Radio Four panel show *I'm Sorry I Haven't A Clue* have been collecting them for entry into the Uxbridge English Dictionary. Some of the most groanworthy definitions are the Yorkshire-isms created by Barry Cryer and Tim Brooke-Taylor. Here are a selection of the best, plus one or two new definitions.

earache Yorkshire expression of surprise at seeing a garden implement

Edam mild Yorkshire expletive

ego Yorkshire for "get lost"

ejaculate Yorkshire greeting to husband on delayed return from t' mill

emit Yorkshire expression of pleasure on finding a lost glove

Kirby grip North Yorkshire handshake

retard very difficult in Yorkshire

surrogate stand-in Yorkshire spa town

tall what's near the front door in Yorkshire

tape measure a device for calculating the size of primates

terminology the study of Yorkshire fur

terse what you see at a funeral

tissues important matters in Yorkshire

toil hole

toilet small hole

towel rail where Yorkshire people keep their owls

trifle Yorkshire gun

trump favourite Yorkshire steak

twee what Yorkshire tea turns into

twig Yorkshireman's toupee

twirled Yorkshire

A local newspaper vendor was standing on the corner of a windswept street in a bustling Yorkshire city centre, shouting, "Read all about it! Twenty-five people cheated! Twenty-five people cheated!" Intrigued, a passer-by bought a paper and glanced down the front page. To his disgust, what he saw was yesterday's news. "Oi! This is yesterday's paper – where's the story about a big swindle?" The newspaper seller ignored him and began crying out, "Read all about it! Twenty-six people cheated!"

One Shrove Tuesday a Bridlington mother was preparing pancakes for her sons, Kevin, five, and Ernie, four. The siblings began to argue over who would get the first. Spotting an opportunity for a moral lesson, their mother told them, "If Jesus were sitting here, he would say, 'Let my brother have the first pancake, I can wait'." Quick as a flash, Kevin turned to his younger brother and said, "Ernie, you be Jesus."

Stan keeps a record of everythin' 'e eats. It's called a tie.

Bill spent a miserable day fly-fishing on the River Wharfe. After hours sitting in the driving rain without making a single catch, he trudged mournfully back to his car and headed for home. On his way, he stopped at a fishmonger's and asked for some trout. "Pick two big 'uns and chuck 'em at me, will you?"

"Why do you want me to throw them at you?" the fishmonger asked, bemused.

"Because I'm going to tell the missus that I caught them," came the reply, accompanied by a knowing wink.

"Okay, but I would go for the salmon," the friendly fishmonger recommended.

"Why's that?" the angler asked.

"Because your wife popped in earlier and said that when I saw you I should tell you to buy salmon, 'cos she fancies that for tea tonight."

Did you hear about the archaeologist who turned down the chance to unearth the skeleton of Richard III? His career's in ruins.

Long after the bells of Big Ben have struck twelve on New Year's Eve, Ronald decides to head home. As he is in no shape to drive, Ronald opts to leave his car and walk – or rather stagger – from the pub. As he weaves along the road, he is stopped by a policeman. "What are you doing out 'ere at four in the morning?" demands the officer. "Ah'm on mi way to a lecture," Ronald replies. "And who in their right mind is going to give a lecture at this time on New Year's Day?" enquires the constable. "Who does tha think?" Ronald slurs. "Mi wife."

A mother was telling her little girl about her own childhood, growing up on a farm in the North York Moors. "We used to skate outside on a pond in the winter and build dams on the beck at the bottom of the field in the summer. I made a swing from some binder twine and an old plank, and it hung from a tree beside the house. Then we would play hide-and-seek and pick gooseberries in the woods." The little girl was wide-eyed and clearly impressed. At last she said, "Wow, I wish I could have got to know you sooner!"

A young boy is asked by his mother to say grace before he tucks into his Sunday dinner. The youngster thanks God for his friends at school.

Then he thanks God for Mummy, Daddy, brother, sister, Nanna, Grandpa and the two dogs.

Next he begins to thank God for the food on the table. He gives thanks for the roast beef, the Yorkshire puddings, the potatoes and the gravy.

Then the boy suddenly stops, raises his eyes from the table, and asks, "Mummy, if I thank God for the sprouts, won't he know I'm lying?"

Buzz, a brash New York tourist, was visiting Middleham to see the castle where Richard III passed his formative years.

After a while spent studying the ruins, the young tourist glanced at his watch and realised he was running late for a play he was due to see in York that evening.

Spotting a tweed-clad chap leaning on a nearby gate, facing away from him, Buzz went over and rather rudely prodded him in the back, "Hey, there! What's the quickest way to Old York?"

"Is tha drivin' or walkin', lad?" came the reply.

"I'm driving," drawled Buzz.

The chap by the gate nodded sagely. "Aye lad, that's certainly t' quickest way."

A tourist is browsing the shelves at a store in Grassington when he spots a sign that reads,

"Danger, beware of the dog". Turning around, he sees an ancient old mongrel flat out on the ground, snoring loudly. Bemused, he asks the shopkeeper, "Is that harmless old mutt what folk are meant to beware of?" "Aye," the shopkeeper nods solemnly. "Afore I put up that sign, people kept trippin' owa 'im."

A hiker is out walking in the wilds of upper Teesdale when thick clouds descend. Before long he realises he is completely lost. As he is about to call for help, the walker stumbles upon a house with a light in the window. A kindly old man invites him inside and urges him to sit by the open range. While the friendly host sorts him a bowl of soup, the walker notes a number of farm animals wandering free around the living room. As the hiker gratefully downs his steaming-hot soup, a little pig pays him particular attention; running to and from his chair, squealing loudly. "My, he's a friendly chap," observes the walker. "Oh, he's not that friendly," comes the reply. "It's just that you're using his bowl."

"My idea o' spring cleanin' is ter sweep t' room wi' a glance."

It was spelling test time at a primary school in the Dales. Farmer's son Ernie was asked by his teacher to spell the word "straight". Little Ernie did so without error.

"Well done!" beamed the teacher. "Now, Ernie, can you tell me what it means?"

Quick as a flash, Ernie's hand shot up. "Without water in it," he replied.

A Dales farmer's beloved cat falls ill and he takes it to the vet for advice. Leaving the pet in a basket in his Land Rover, he pops into the surgery.

"Reet then, vitnary, Ah need to talk to thee abaht mi cat. It's bin actin' strangely." "Well then, Mr Birkbeck, is it a tom?" the vet asks.

"Nay lad, Ah've browt it wi' us."

A London banker was tootling along a winding road in the North York Moors when his sports car spluttered to a standstill near a field filled with Swaledale sheep. The driver got out and lifted the bonnet of the car to investigate the problem. As he scratched his head in puzzlement, he noticed one of the sheep was looking at him.

"Ah would say it'll be yer cambelt," the sheep bleated in a broad Yorkshire accent.

The man nearly jumped out of his pinstripes. He ran to a nearby farmhouse and knocked on the door.

"One of your sheep just told me what was wrong with my car," he shouted excitedly.

The farmer leaned out of the doorway. "T' tup wi' 'alf a horn missin'?" he asked.

"Yes, that's it... I think," the man replied.

"Aye, well. That'd be Derek. Tek nae notice o' 'im, 'e knows nowt abaht cars."

Five-year-old Jessica and her little brother Daniel were sitting together in a church pew at a family wedding in Skipton. Daniel kept giggling and talking loudly, much to his big sister's annoyance. Finally she had had enough and hissed under her breath, "You're not supposed to make a noise in church."

"Who's going to stop me?" Daniel asked.

Jessica pointed to the back of the church and said, "See those two grown-ups standing by the door? Dad says they're hushers."

A Keighley man's beloved collie, Ben, dies of old age and as it was such a big part of his life for so long, the heartbroken pensioner resolves to have a gold statue made by a jeweller in Bradford to remember his pet by.

"Reet then, can tha mek us a gold statue of our owd dog?" the man asks the jeweller.

"I should think so. Do you want it to be eighteen carat?" comes the reply.

"Eh?" exclaims the man. "Nay, Ah want it chewin' a bone, tha daft apeth."

Little Jimmy went up to Old Ron the gardener with a quizzical look on his face. "What do you put on your rhubarb?" he asked. "Well, Ah usually go for 'orse manure," came the reply. Jimmy looked surprised. "Oh, right," he said. "We have custard".

At a pub quiz in a Dales hostelry it has reached a tie-break, with nothing to separate two of the regulars. The duo are told that the winner will be the first to name three fish beginning with the letter K. After a moment's hesitation, one of the men replies, "Killer shark, kippered herring and Kettlewell." "What do you mean? Kettlewell isn't a fish," the landlord exclaims. "Aye, 'tis," the man retorts, "'tis a place."

A father was on the beach at Scarborough with his two children when his four-year-old son, David, ran up to him, grabbed him by the hand and led him to the shoreline, where a seagull lay dead in the sand.

"Daddy, what happened to that bird?" David asked.

"He died and went to heaven," his dad replied diplomatically.

The boy thought a moment and then said, "Did God throw him back down?"

A man visiting the zoo at Flamingo Land asks a passing keeper, "Eyup lad, 'as tha no talkin' parrots?" "No," says the keeper, "but we have got a woodpecker that knows Morse code."

A man is halfway through his stay at a Scarborough hotel when he goes to the reception desk and rings the bell. "Can I help you, sir?" asks the receptionist. "Well, the card in my room said I should alert the management of any complaints," explains the holidaymaker. "That's correct, sir," says the receptionist.
What's the matter?" "Oh, not much," says the guest, "just a touch of arthritis and a dodgy knee."

A visitor to the Whitby Goth Weekend, dressed as Dracula, is busily rearranging chairs that have been set up at Whitby Abbey. "What are you up to?" asks a curious fellow festival-goer. "Not much," says the caped reveller. "I'm just doing a bit of Fang-Shui."

A West Yorkshire city disappeared off the map earlier today. Police are looking for Leeds.

Husband: "Fetch thi coat, lass, Ah'm off ter t' pub. Tha'll need ter wrap up wahm."

Wife: "Oh, that's nice Stan, tha's not tekken me out for years."

Husband: "Nay, tha's not coming wi' me, lass – Ah'm turnin' t' heating off when Ah leave!"

"Do you know when I realised I loved her? When she came to our house and ate a full Yorkshire pudding, gravy and all. She eats like a horse. I thought: 'She is the girl for me'."

Michael Parkinson on his wife Mary

Five-year-old Fiona is sitting quietly in a pew at her first wedding. When the bride and groom have left the church, she turns to her mother and whispers, "Why did the lady change her mind?" Surprised, her mother asks, "What do you mean?" "Well," explains Fiona, "she walked down the aisle with one man and came back with a different one."

Nev and Kev are supping pints on a mid-January evening at a Beverley pub when Nev asks Kev for a cigarette.

"I thought tha'd quit fer New Year," says Kev.

"That's right," replies Nev. "I'm in the process of giving up. Right now, I'm in the middle of phase one," he explains.

"Oh, reet, Ah see," says Kev. "What's this phase one?"

"Well," says Nev, "I've quit buying."

A southerner is chatting with his northern friend on the telephone.

"I met a chap from Yorkshire yesterday," he remarks conversationally.

"How do you know he was from Yorkshire?" asks the northerner.

"Erm, well, he sounded like he was."

"So he didn't tell you he was a Yorkshireman?"

"Well, no, he didn't," the southerner admits.

"Then he wasn't from Yorkshire."

'Excellent' in every catergory

When inspectors gave Sheffield High School a glowing report, staff were understandably proud. However, a sign installed in the school grounds to celebrate the success (above) did not exactly help.

Campers? They are nature's way o' feedin' t' midges.

A rambler in the North York Moors spots an old chap standing beside a drystone wall, holding a short length of binder twine at arm's length. "What's the bit of string for?" asks the curious rambler. "Ah, well, it's an owd country way Ah use fer tellin' t' weather," the old man replies. "So how does it work?" asks the rambler, fascinated. "Well," the elderly sage replies earnestly. "When t' twine swings abaht it's windy, an' when it gets wet it's fair silin' it dahn."

Little Billy had been chosen to play one of the Wise Men in his school nativity and he proudly devised his own costume. Walking into the school assembly hall, his friend and fellow Wise Man, Timmy, spotted him and ran over, looking confused. "Billy, why are you wearing a fireman's helmet?" he asked. "Cos in t' Bible it says 't' three Wise Men came from a fire'."

"I became a great runner
because if you're a kid in Leeds and your
name is Sebastian you've got to become a great
runner."

Sebastian Coe

"Kilburn White Horse in the North Yorkshire Moors looks as though it has been drawn by a group of five-year-olds who have discovered which drawer their teacher keeps his vodka in."

Hugh Dennis, *Britty Britty Bang Bang*

"My local curry house does a reet good chicken korma, tha knows – it proper tickles the tastebuds," remarks Barry over a pint. "Oh aye, what's their secret?" his pal asks. "Well, Ah've heard," says Barry conspiratorially, "that they leave t' feathers on."

"The weather will be
brighter in the north than the south -
like the people."

Brian Redhead

The quarry manager called old William into his
office to break the news that he thought it
was time for him to retire after more than
sixty years with the company. Bill was most
indignant.

"So it's come to this, 'as it? Ah'm not wanted
any longer? Ah worked for thi dad, thi granddad
an' 'is dad an all, tha knows. Ah tell thi what,
lad, if Ah'd known this job weren't permanent,
Ah'd nivver 'ave tekken it on."

A customer walks angrily into a Leeds second-hand shop, brandishing a woollen rug.

"Ey, lad, tha sold mi this rug this morning an' it's got a great big hole in t' middle o' it."

"That's right," says the shopkeeper calmly. "If you recall, I told you it was 'in mint condition'."

Sign above a pub bar in a remote dale: "Due to the recent water shortage, ale will now be served at full strength."

An ageing Yorkshireman undergoes a groundbreaking operation to improve his hearing. Doctors at a hospital in Leeds give him a pig's ear transplant – the first of its kind in the world.

Several weeks later, the patient is back at hospital for a check-up. "Any problems?" asks the doctor.

"Nay doctor, it's fine," says the man. "Though from time to time, I do get a bit o' crackling."

Robert Mugabe has Yorkshire roots. Try saying his surname backwards.

"When judging southerners, we must always remember that they have not had the benefit of our disadvantages."

Harry Pearson

Little Ernie is talking to his granddad. "Why does it rain?" he asks. "To make the plants grow," Granddad replies. Puzzled, the boy asks, "So why does it rain on the pavement?"

A man walks into a Whitby fish shop and barks, "Fish 'n' chips twice please." To which, the man behind the counter replies, "Ah 'eard you t' first time."

Q: What did the dalesman say when he heard the Tour de France was coming to Yorkshire? A: "Nowt so queer as spokes."

Octogenarian Dickie Bird, the world's most famous umpire and a bestselling author, was waiting to meet up with some chums outside the newly opened Barnsley Experience, the museum based at the imposing town hall. They were all off for a cup of tea in the nearby café. He may be getting on, but when a passing fan asked him if he was also planning to have a look around the museum, he showed that his sense of fun had not diminished. "Nay lad," he said with a twinkle in those beady eyes. "I'm getting so old and slow on my feet now that if I go into a place like that I'm afraid that they might take me for a dummy, have me dressed up as an exhibit, and I'll never ever get out again!"

It is the early hours of Boxing Day morning and Bill, Freda and their two children are fast asleep at their Wensleydale home, sleeping off an exhausting family Christmas.

Suddenly, the parents are woken from their deep slumber by a loud knocking at the front door.

Bill grabs his dressing gown and staggers down the stairs, still slightly unsteady from the previous day's feasting. He opens the door and finds a drunk on his doorstep.

"'Appy Chrrrissshmash," slurs the man.

"And to you," snaps Bill, "but can I help you?"

"Well Ah jush wondered if you could give me a push," comes the reply.

"No," grunts Bill. "Don't you know what time it is?" and he slams the door shut. Having headed back upstairs to bed, Bill tells Freda what the man wanted.

"You mean you left him out in the snow at Christmas with a broken-down motor? Get out there and help him push his car."

"But he's drunk, and he shouldn't be driving anyway," protests Bill.

"Well, then that's all the more reason to help him,

isn't it?" insists Freda, shoving her husband out from under the duvet.

Muttering under his breath, Bill struggles into some clothes and heads back outside into the freezing cold.

"Do you still want a push?" he shouts into the darkness.

"Aye, that'd be grand," comes the reply. "Ah'm over 'ere on your swing."

Husband: "I've made the chicken soup." Wife: "Thank goodness, I thought it was our tea."

"In't that Valentine's Day grand?" said Ernie over a pint of Landlord. "Well, Ah nivver 'ad you down as a romantic," remarked a surprised Fred. "Aye well, it's t' day after Ah like, ter be 'onest," admitted Ernie. "That's when they 'ave all them chocolates on sale at 'alf price."

SITUATED in an attractive cul-de-sac and overlooking a corpse is this modern family property.

The quality accommodation includes gas central heating and double glazing throughout, featuring a 21ft lounge, guest cloakroom, dining room, den, luxury fitted breakfast kitchen, en suite master bedroom, three further bedrooms and bathroom.

The house stands amid properties of a similar standard on a popular development in Alwoodley, and there are good local facilities within easy

Well, here's a unique selling point. This cutting from the property section of a local paper describes a property for sale in Alwoodley, Leeds. Would you be brave enough to move there?

Teacher: "Who can tell me the name of the Speaker of the House?" Pupil: "Mummy."

Leisure centre winner is Steve

The winner of a competition to name the new leisure centre in Selby is Steve Wadsworth.

He has won a free year's membership from Wigan Leisure and Culture Trust (WLCT).

He chose the name 'Selby Leisure Centre'.

The new facility will open in the spring at the site of the old Abbey Leisure Centre.

A customer orders a cup of coffee in a Bradford café, takes a mouthful, then promptly spits it out in disgust. "'Ere, love, there's muck in this coffee," he shouts at the waitress.

"That's right, sir," comes the reply. "It were ground only a few hours ago."

In these austere times for local authorities, the construction of a new leisure centre is rightly big news. Therefore excitement was surely mounting in Selby, North Yorkshire, where a replacement for the old Abbey Leisure Centre was being constructed. But what to call this fantastic new centre? Selby District Council decided to ask members of the public to come up with some suggestions. The exciting result was announced with fanfare in local paper the *Selby Times*.

Why won't you ever find a witch wearing a flat cap? Because there's no point.

Woman talking to another about men: "Afore yer married 'e'll lift thee ower a puddle, but after 'e'll look around ter see if tha's fallen in t' beck."

Pupil: "Ah'll 'ave roast beef an' Yorksher puddin'." Dinner lady: "Isn't there a word you've forgotten?" Pupil: "Oh, aye, Ah nearly forgot – gravy."

A devoutly religious Dales farmer had for many years carried a precious yet dog-eared copy of the Book of Common Prayer with him each day as he worked in the fields. One day, while mending a section of drystone wall, he lost the book, only noticing when he returned to the farmhouse. Hastily retracing his steps, he could find no sign of it. Several weeks later, having given up all hope of finding the sacred tome, a Swaledale sheep approached him, carrying an object in its mouth that looked decidedly familiar. It was the missing prayer book. The normally reserved chap's jaw dropped open. "'Tis a miracle!" he exclaimed. "Not really," replied the sheep. "Your name's written inside the cover."

Which football team do fans of Yorkshire cheese support? Sheffield Wensleydale.

A new teacher was taking her first arithmetic class at a small primary school in the Dales. "Just suppose," she asked the class, "that there were thirty sheep in a field, and that eight of them jumped over the wall. How many would be left?"

Little Carl put up his hand and said "None". The teacher frowned. "None? Carl, you don't know your arithmetic." Carl replied: "Miss, tha don't know thi Yorkshire sheep. When yan goes, they all go!"

YORKSHIRE AT T' PICTURES

Yorkshire is the birthplace of some of the greatest names ever to grace the silver screen – Judi Dench, Sean Bean, Patrick Stewart, James Mason, Ben Kingsley, Mr Tickle... the list just goes on and on.

Yet, with the glorious exception of *Wetherby* (1986, starring Vanessa Redgrave, Ian Holm and Judi Dench – Google it!), there are scandalously few films with proper Yorkshire titles. To put matters right, here are a few suggestions...

LORD OF THE PICKERINGS

A FEW GOOD MENSTON

MORLEY AND ME

BAWTRY AND THE BEAST

THE GOOD, THE BRADFORD AND THE ILKLEY

SUMMAT ALL FEARS

ATTACK OF THE LUDDENDENFOOT WOMAN

RESERVOIR CLOGS

REETH ENCOUNTER

BECK TO T' FUTURE

THE GRAPES OF WATH

BEVERLEY HULL COP

HELLO, DONNY!

BRING ME THE HEADINGLEY
OF AMY GARCIA

LETHAL RIPON

PLANET OF THE DAFT APETHS

DIRTY HARROGATE

KNOTTINGLEY HILL

LOOK OUSE TALKING

THE FRED TRUEMAN SHOW

FAR FROM THE ADDINGHAM CROWD

SHALLOW GRAVY

PENNINES FROM HEAVEN

FORREST EE BAH GUMP

GUISELEY AND DOLLS

SOME LIKE IT OTLEY

LAYER BREADCAKE

HIS GOOLE FRIDAYTHORPE

RAGING HULL

JURASSIC PARKIN

DRIFFIELD OF DREAMS

EEEEEEE.T.

LIFE OF PIE

ELLAND THAT TIME FORGOT

Depending on where you're from, "Mamma Mia" is either a classic Abba song or a lad telling his mother he's back home.

What do you call a Yorkshireman who refuses a drink on his birthday? Dead.

"What's that perfume you're wearing, Nurse Gladys Emmanuel? 'Evening in Plaster-of-Paris', isn't it?" – *Arkwright, Open All Hours*

Christmas in't what it was. When Ah were a lad, t' family huddled around t' coal fire on Christmas Eve... an' if it got reight, reight cowd, we'd light it.

Screen Break

Compo Simmonite: I could murder some fish and chips.

Foggy Dewhurst: You usually do.

Norman Clegg: If ever there's been a neglected subject in poetry, it's vinegar.

Last of the Summer Wine

T' NAME'S BOND.
JIM BOND...

At the time of writing, seven actors have portrayed James Bond on film. There's been a Scotsman, an Irishman, a Welshman and even an Australian, but never a Yorkshireman.

Before the film studios put this travesty right, here are some film suggestions for a Yorkie Bond:

DR NOWT

FROM RUSHOLME WITH LOVE

GOLD FINGALL

DIAMONDS ARE FOR ELSECAR

T' MAN WI' T' GOLDEN GUNNERSIDE

MOOK-RAKER

T' SPY WHO LOVED MEAT PIES

FOR YOUR PIES HONLEY

OTLEYPUSSY

NIVVER SAY NIVVER AGAIN

A VIEW TO A GILL

LICENCE TO KILLINGHALL

GOLCAR AYE

TODMORDEN NIVVER DIES

THE WOLDS IS NOT ENOUGH

56

"The thing with high-tech is that you always end up using scissors."

David Hockney

A Yorkshire aerobics instructor was leading her fitness group in some exercises. "Right then," she said, "hands on thighs." They all did as they were told. None of them could see a thing.

Overheard at a market stall: an elderly woman was returning a four-pack of toilet rolls she had bought earlier that week, demanding a refund. "Why, what's wrong wi' 'em?" asked the stallholder. "Nowt," came the reply, "but the posh folk what was comin' to ours nivver turned up and we can't afford ter use bog roll that good."

A man rang his friend and said, "Oh, I've been to a fabulous restaurant – the music, the ambience, the food, the service – fabulous!" His friend asked, "What was it called?" He replied, "It was called the, er – oh, what's the name of that tall, thin plant with thorns and a flower on the top?" His friend said, "Rose?" He said, "Rose... what was the name of that restaurant we went to?" – *Maureen Lipman*

I just hope this re-enactment of the burial of Richard III helps them catch the blokes that did it.

The schoolteacher frowned at little Alfie. "It's butter, not booter," she said. The young lad puzzled for a moment before putting up his hand. "What is it?" the teacher asked. "Please, Miss," said Alfie. "What do I say for jam?"

We were a big
family, an' we couldn't afford
turkey back then. Mam used ter
buy an octopus – that way we
could all 'ave a leg.

Money talks... but all mine ever says is "ta-ra".

Here's a good money-saving Yorkshire alternative
to asparagus – in 1953 a Nidderdale newspaper
reported, "If young, curly, four-inch-long bracken
shoots are boiled in slightly salted water and served
with butter, they taste like asparagus and make a
very tasty dish." There was a letter in the following
week's edition: "I have tried boiled bracken and
cannot recommend it."

Ah don't like
seein' t' bairns go hungry
on Christmas Day. Teks all t'
enjoyment out o' eatin' thi own
Christmas dinner.

A visitor to a hotel in Scarborough was asked at breakfast how he would like his eggs cooked. "I want one so hard that it would bounce, and the other so soft that I could drink it with a straw," he replied. "I'm not sure we can manage that," said the waiter. "Why not?" came the reply. "Tha did it yesterday."

One late afternoon, a Leeds man is staggering home after an all-day session at his local hostelry. On his winding way he spots a man from the water board with a large T-shaped handle opening a valve at the bottom of a manhole. He walks up to the workman and gives him a shove. "Oi, what were that fer?" asks the indignant engineer. "That's fer tunnin' all t' streets roun' when Ah'm tryin' ter find mi way home."

A husband and wife are on a camping trip in the Dales. After a long day's hiking in beautiful sunshine, the couple pitch their tent in a stunning part of Wensleydale and, utterly exhausted, they soon fall sound asleep.

In the middle of the night, awoken by the screech of a passing owl, the woman shakes her husband's shoulder to wake him also.

"John, look up," she says. "What do you see?"

"Well, I see thousands of stars," he says sleepily. "What a beautiful sky."

"And what does that mean to you?" his wife asks.

"Well, I suppose it means we are in for another nice day tomorrow. What does it mean to you?"

"Well, John," she replies, "to me, it means someone's stolen our tent."

"I'm from Yorkshire. I'm the full Brontë." –
Barry Cryer

Ted: "Ah took wife ter see a stand-up comedian fer 'er birthday last week."

Bob: "Jimmy Carr?"

Ted: "Nay lad, she wanted ter go."

"Who would have thought that big, fat Yorkshire pudding would become such a twinkletoes?"
– *Len Goodman*, Strictly Come Dancing *judge,
on Darren Gough*

> "People say I'm the son of God, but it isn't true – my Nigel is."
>
> *Brian Clough*

Two walkers, intently studying a map, are passed by a farm worker near Yockenthwaite in Langstrothdale.

"Excuse me, sir, can you tell us what this place is called?" one of the walkers asks.

"Yoc-n-thw-t," comes the reply.

"Could you say that again?"

"Yoc-n-thw-t."

"Erm, could you spell it?"

The farm man pauses and scratches his head, before replying, "They do-an't spell it; they nobbut say it."

Scarborough Borough Council
St Hilda's Terrace Permit

Please indicate below and return this form to the Parking Services Department, The Town Hall, St Nicholas Street, Scarborough. YO

If this form is not returned before 30 April 2015 it will be assumed purchase a Full Annual Permit and it will be offered to the next pe applicable. Please indicate which type of permit you require and a

❏ I would like to purchase a St Hildas Terrace Permit at a co

❏ I enclose a cheese made payable to Scarborough Borough payment

Drivers in Whitby received a generous offer from Scarborough Borough Council – pay for your parking permit with cheese!

Old John, hurrying towards the railway station, was overtaken by a younger neighbour. "Hey Fred," he called, "will ta book me a return ticket?"

"Wheer to?" asked Fred.

"Back 'ere, yer fooil," replied John.

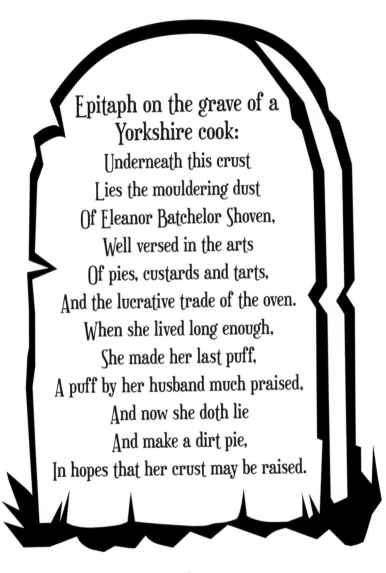

Epitaph on the grave of a
Yorkshire cook:
Underneath this crust
Lies the mouldering dust
Of Eleanor Batchelor Shoven,
Well versed in the arts
Of pies, custards and tarts,
And the lucrative trade of the oven.
When she lived long enough,
She made her last puff,
A puff by her husband much praised,
And now she doth lie
And make a dirt pie,
In hopes that her crust may be raised.

A Dales vicar is offering one of his parishioners some spiritual advice.

"You know, my man," he says, "one far greater than either of us notices everything we do."

"Yes, Reverend," replies the man. "She's already spoken to me about it."

T'was t' neet
afore Christmas 'n all thrurr
t' 'ouse,
Not a creature wur stirrin',
not even a mouse.
T' stockings were 'ung by t'
chimney wi' care.
They'd bin worn arl week, 'n
needed t' air.

One wintry afternoon, young Jim and John were skating on a large frozen puddle that took up much of a Nidderdale field. A farmer and sheepdog, herding a flock of sheep, decided to take a shortcut across the frozen area. The sheep, however, were afraid of the ice and wouldn't cross it. Annoyed, the farmer began dragging them across. "Look at that," remarked Jim to John. "That bloke's tryin' ter pull t' wool over our ice!"

What do you call a group of chess grand masters bragging about their successes in the lobby of Scarborough's Grand Hotel? Chess nuts boasting in an open foyer.

Reporter: "Will you buy your wife a present?"

"Maybe I'll let her have a look in the Argos catalogue."

Hull's £20million lottery winner Terry Benson

Two strangers are sitting at a bus stop in Otley.

"What's tha do fer a livin'?" asks one.

"Ah'm a bit of a wheeler-dealer," comes the reply.

"Sounds interesting. Picked up any bargains lately?"

"Well, today Ah were at a clearance sale for a pub that's closed down in Ilkley – more bar tat."

"My New Year's resolution is to be more optimistic by keeping my glass half-full – of Old Peculier."

Gateways D of E

@gwaysdofe

Twitter account of Gateways School Duck of Edinburgh award scheme. One of only two schools in Yorkshire & Humber granted a local operating license.

📍 Harewood, Leeds

Who knew there was an awards scheme named after a royal waterfowl?

On the morning of New Year's Eve, Sarah told her boyfriend John, "Ah just 'ad a dream where you got daahn on one knee in front o' me at t' stroke o' midnight – what dost tha think it means? Ah woke up just afowa things got interesting." "Aha, tha'll knaw terneet," answered John, smiling broadly. At midnight, as Big Ben chimed, John approached Sarah and handed her a small parcel. Delighted and excited, she opened it quickly. There in her hands rested a book entitled *The Meaning of Dreams*.

"I was criticised for swearing on television. The word I used was 'bloody', which, where I come from in Yorkshire, is practically the only surviving adjective."

Maureen Lipman

An assistant at a Leeds department store spotted a chap looking lost, just before closing time. "I want to buy some Christmas presents," the shopper said. "When are your opening hours?"

The shop assistant replied, "I'm not opening yours, I'm opening mine!"

A husband and wife are standing at the window admiring their garden. "Sooner or later tha's goin' ter 'ave ter mek a proper scarecrow ter keep t' birds off," says the wife. "What's wrong wi' t' one we've got?" asks the husband. "Nowt," replies his wife. "But Mam's arms are gettin' tired."

> "If it wasn't for Emmerdale I wouldn't get any fresh air at all."
>
> *John Cooper Clarke*

The new boss of a Dales quarry was concerned about the welfare of his staff working through bleak winter conditions, so he bought them all earmuffs.

"What's these?" asked Tom, one of his staff, suspiciously.

"They're to keep your ears warm," replied his boss.

Grudgingly, Tom put them on. A day later, however, the manager noticed that Tom wasn't wearing the earmuffs even though the temperature had dropped still further.

"Didn't you like the earmuffs?" he asked. "It's Baltic out here."

"Them blasted things!" Tom exclaimed. "Ah wur wearin' them t' fust day, an' somebody offered to buy me a pint, but Ah didn't hear him! Never again, never again!"

"Ah don't like this 'ere new-fangled anorak," a rambler grumbled to his friend. "Why, wot's wrong wi' it?" came the reply. "It's this 'ere Velcro fastening," said the rambler. "What a rip-off!"

Genuine questions asked by guests at Sheffield's Travelodge: "Can you fill my bath with exactly 100 litres of Evian water at a temperature of 38 degrees?"; "Do the footballers only play today?" (it was a Wednesday).

A man walks into a Holmfirth pub and orders a triple brandy and a double whisky chaser.

"You know, I shouldn't really be drinking this with what I've got," says the man to the barman, as he downs the first drink in one.

"Why? What have you got?" asks the barman.

"Nobbut fifty pence."

"Ah can't believe Ah were sacked from t' calendar printers. All Ah did were tek a day off."

"Ah wouldn't say Harry's tight, but Ah went round there t' other day an' found 'im stripping t' wallpaper. 'E's not decorating, 'e's movin' 'ouse."

"T' secret o' 'appiness – good 'ealth and a bad memory."

What do you call a newborn Swaledale lamb covered in mud? A Yorkie chocolate baa.

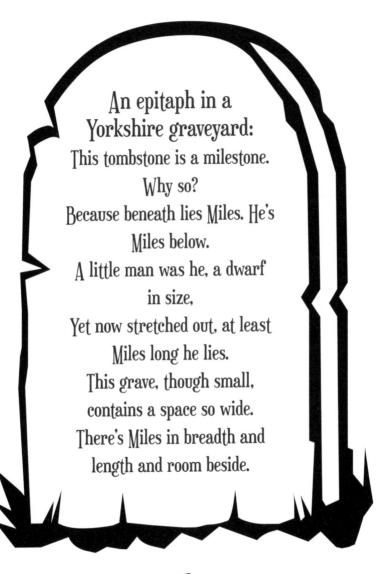

An epitaph in a
Yorkshire graveyard:
This tombstone is a milestone.
Why so?
Because beneath lies Miles. He's
Miles below.
A little man was he, a dwarf
in size,
Yet now stretched out, at least
Miles long he lies.
This grave, though small,
contains a space so wide.
There's Miles in breadth and
length and room beside.

Tyke Times

The lighter side of the news

The art of the headline writer is sadly dying out, which is a real shame because when they are at their best, a newspaper headline can be laugh-out-loud funny. Here's a selection of Yorkshire gems.

When Leeds-born playwright Alan Bennett published his diaries, they proved immensely popular, even outselling a book by the Pope. *The Times*' witty response was:

God and Bennett

When rival bra manufacturers competed over who could make the brassiere with the greatest uplift, the *Yorkshire Post*'s business pages reported:

Twin piques as firms try to lift profit figures

The male striptease troupe Chippendales were causing a sensation wherever they performed. The *York Press* cleverly punned:

Good biceps, Mister Chipps

When Yorkshire Coast Radio wanted to let the organisers of local events know that it was happy to promote them on air, it made the announcement in the *Scarborough Evening News* under the headline:

Your fete is our destiny

A singles club in Doncaster was in danger of closure after more than half of the members had paired off, resulting in four successive weddings. The *Guardian* headline writer's take on the story was:

Four weddings could mean club's funeral

The arrival of a new creamery in Yorkshire would provide a welcome jobs boost for the county. The *Yorkshire Post*'s headline was:

What a friend we have in cheeses

Middlesbrough Borough Council's decision to cut back on toilet rolls in public conveniences was reported by the *Sunday Sun* with this headline:

A-tissue, a-tissue, we're four rolls down

A feature in the *Yorkshire Post*'s agricultural pages explained new techniques for fattening pigs. Apparently you talk to them. The headline was:

Chat up a pig... and see the last of the slimmer swine

An organisation dedicated to clowns was searching for a new home for its archives and memorabilia after being kicked out of its old base. The *Yorkshire Post* told us:

Homeless clowns loiter within tent

Guided tours were being offered around the ancient and modern lavatories of York. The *Liverpool Daily Echo*'s response was the clever headline:

Now it's to loos le trek

When the £25 million Bourbon Street redevelopment in Sheffield ran into trouble, the *Sheffield Telegraph* headlined their story:

Bourbon on the rocks

Image credits

Pearls (p2): BSGStudio; sign (pages 8, 12, 37): freedesignfile; cassette tape (p10): BSGStudio; records (p11): Keistutis; clapper board (pages 15, 53): freedesignfile; ice skate (p21): johnny_automatic; Brussels sprouts (p22): GDJ; holly (pages 52, 59, 60, 66, 71): BSGStudio; picture frame (p56): freedesignfile; gravestone (pages 65, 75): gloomus
All other images © Country Publications Ltd